Parks, Trails In th St. Louis Area And Selected Parts of Missouri

Compiled by: Dr. Michael Stachiw

Photos contributed by: Brandon Williams & Jackie Stachiw

Edited by: Cathy Caligiuri

Parks, Trails, & Hikes in the St. Louis Area and Selected Parts of Missouri

Copyright 2016

All rights reserved

Printed in the United States of America

Published by SM&DS through Createspace Independent Publishing Platform

ISBN-13: 978-1533118172

ISBN-10: 1533118175

Copyright © 2016 Dr. Michael Stachiw

All rights reserved, including rights or reproduction and use in any form or by any means. This includes the making of copies, printed, written, oral, or recorded for sound or visual reproduction or for use in any knowledge retrieval system or device, unless permission in writing is obtained from the copyright proprietor.

Table of Contents

Introduction i
Rules, Etiquette, and Safety Tips ii
Bee Tree Park 1
Black Forest Park 5
Bohrer Park 9
Buder Park 13
Castlewood State Park 17
Creve Coeur Lake Memorial Park 22
Dr. Edmund A. Babler Memorial State Park 26
Emmenegger Nature Park 30
Faust Park 34
Fort Belle Fontaine Park 38
Greensfelder Park 42
Laumeier Sculpture Park 46
Lone Elk Park 50
Love Park 54
Mastodon State Park 58
McDonnell Park 62
Montauk State Park 66
Powder Valley Conservation Nature Center 70
Queeny Park 74
Robertsville State Park 79
Route 66 State Park 83
Simpson Park 88
Spanish Lake Park 92
Stacy Park 96
Unger Park 101
West Tyson Park 106
County and State Parks 110
Hiking Equipment Checklist 111

Introduction

Being committee chairman for a few years for my scout troop and helping with various activities required in running a troop, I have participated in many hiking adventures in the St Louis area. Time and time again I have re-hiked these trails either with the troop or on my own. My extensive knowledge and passion for hiking has inspired me to create this guide to help others discover their hiking passion.

Please note that not every park or trail in the St Louis area is covered in this book, just those that I have intimate knowledge of. Also, I did not list those private trails that exist on Scout land and can only be used by registered Boy Scouts and their leaders.

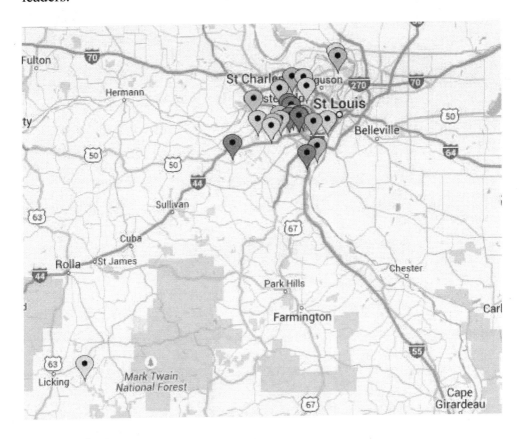

Rules, Etiquette & Safety Tips

Just like any sport, hiking has a set of rules along with generally recognized etiquette to make it safe and enjoyable. Please take a minute to look over these important guidelines:

- Avoid hiking alone. The buddy system is safer, especially when hiking in new locations. If hiking alone, be sure to let someone know where you are going, and when you should be returning.
- Always carry rain gear and return back if weather turns bad. If you become cold, it is imperative to get warm as quickly as possible to avoid hypothermia.
- Stay on marked trails to avoid becoming lost.
- Always carry clean water and drink often to avoid dehydration.
- Carry a whistle that can be heard from far away. Three short blasts is a sign of distress.
- Wear bright colors and do not dress in camouflage, especially children.
- Never rely on your cell phone to work in the wilderness.
- Pack a simple first aid kit and a first aid kit guide, as things do not always go according to plan.

Bee Tree Park

2701 Finestown Road
Saint Louis, MO 63129
(314) 615-4733

Park Hours
- 8 am to one half hour past official sunset.

Lengths
- Mississippi Trail: 0.8 miles
- Crow's Roost Trail: 0.8 miles
- Fisherman's Trail: 0.8 miles
- Paw Paw Trail: 0.5 miles
- Cedar Trail: 0.1 miles

Amenities
- Bathroom
- Shelter
- Scenic Overlook
- Fishing Dock
- Nims Mansion

Fun Fact
- The land was previously owned by Southwestern Bell Telephone Company founder Eugene Nims.

Trails

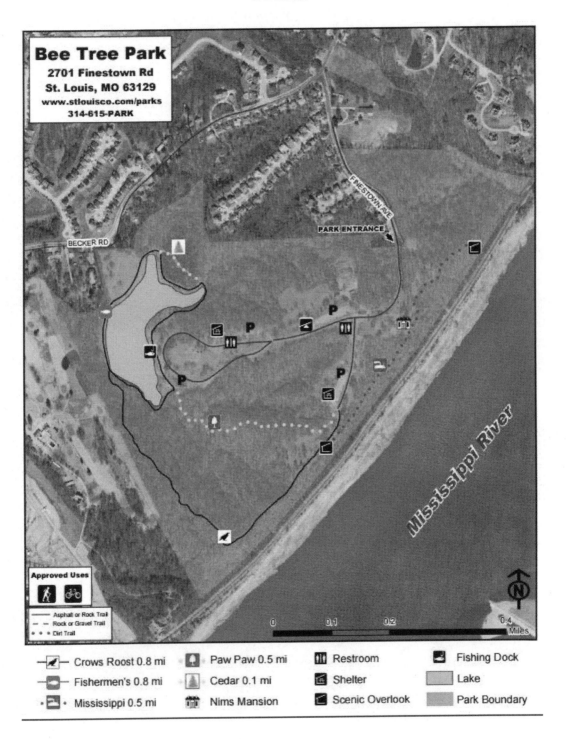

Bee Tree Park Pictures

Signs are posted around the park detailing lake and park rules.

Map

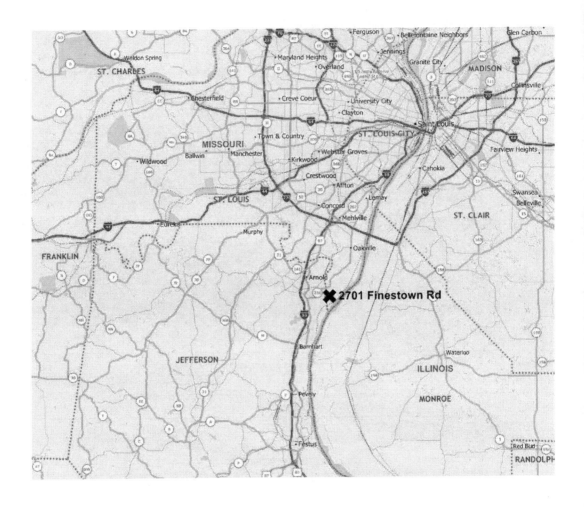

Black Forest Park

9822 Perrin Avenue
Saint Louis, MO 63125

Park Hours
- 8 am to one half hour past official sunset.

Length
- There are no trails in Black Forest Park

Amenities
- Playground
- Basketball Court
- History of Black Forest
- Restroom

Fun Fact
- The park was opened to the public in 1960, and is included in the Mississippi River Greenway.

Amenities

Black Forest Park Pictures

Black Forest Park is a great place for kids to hang out on the playground.

The Black Forest Park sign greets visitors from all around St. Louis.

Map

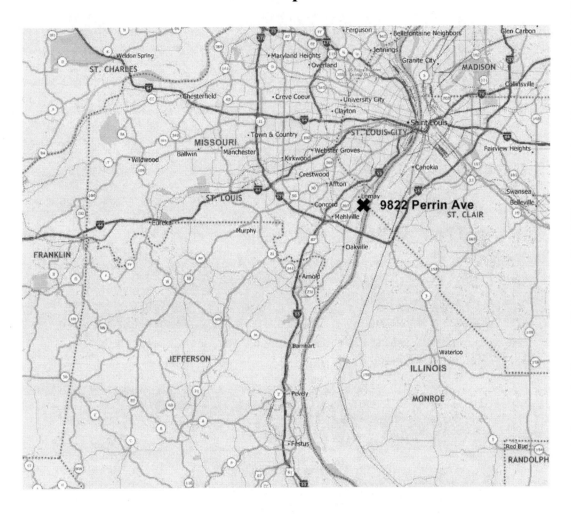

Bohrer Park
5705 South Lindbergh
Saint Louis, MO 63123
(314) 615-4386

Park Hours
- 8 am to one half hour past official sunset.

Length
- There are no trails at Bohrer Park

Amenities
- Playground
- Tennis Courts
- Restroom

Fun Fact
- The park was named in honor of George E. Bohrer, a County Councilman from the 6th district, who served from 1957 until his death in 1960.

Amenities

Bohrer Park Pictures

A pond located in the center of Bohrer, providing beautiful scenery for the entire park.

Bohrer also has two tennis courts near the entrance to the park that are free to use.

Map

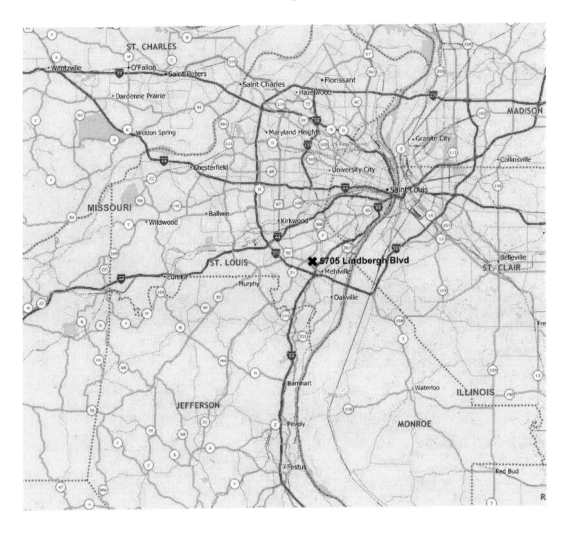

Buder Park
1919 Valley Park Road
Saint Louis, MO 63026
(314) 615-4733

Part of the original land was lost with the construction of Interstate 44, and the park was split into the upper area on the hill, called Buder South, and the lower area close to the river, Buder North.

Park Hours
- 8 am to one half hour after official sunset.

Length
- 1.5 miles

Amenities
Buder (North)
- Archery Range
- RC Airplane fields
- Baseball/Softball fields
- Soccer fields
- Trail

Buder (South)
- Playground
- Picnic Shelter
- Restrooms

Fun Fact
- Buder Park was originally given to the City of St. Louis in 1917 by Gustavus Buder and his wife for use as a swimming beach and other park purposes.

Trail and Amenities

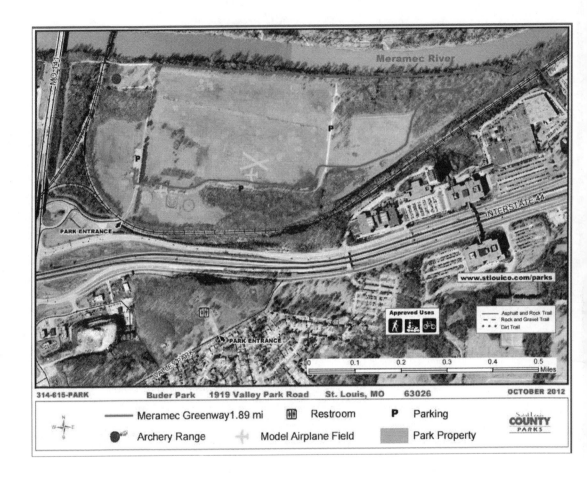

Buder Park Pictures

A large paved trail completely surrounds the entirety of Buder Park.

A playground featured at the park is free for children to use.

Map

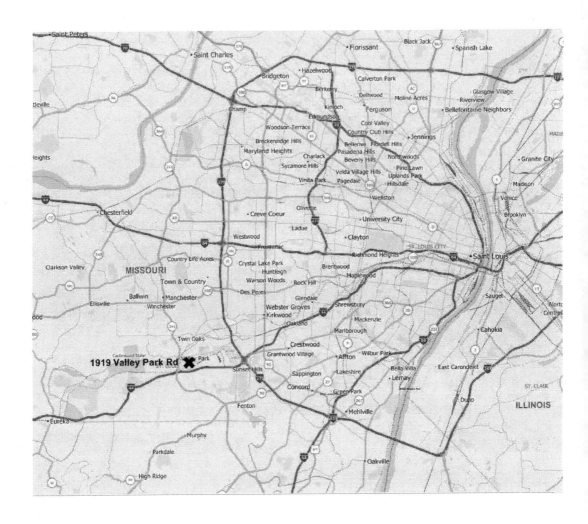

Castlewood State Park
1401 Kiefer Creek Rd
Ballwin, MO 63021
(636) 227-4433

Park hours
- 7 am to one-half hour after sunset, year-round. Park gates open and close at these times.

Lengths
- Lone Wolf Trail: 1.5 miles
- River Scene Trail: 4.3 miles

Amenities
- Restrooms
- Picnic Area
- Shelters

Fun Fact
- This area used to be a hot spot for partying in the St. Louis area in the early 1900s.

Trails

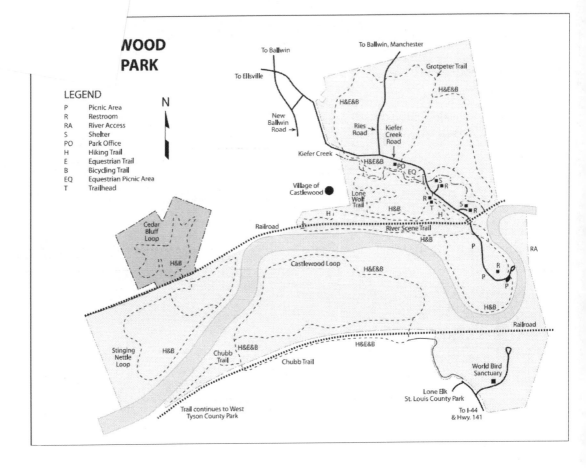

Castlewood State Park Pictures

A delightful gazebo that has a variety of informational flyers on its bulletin board.

One of the many trails featured at Castlewood State Park.

Map

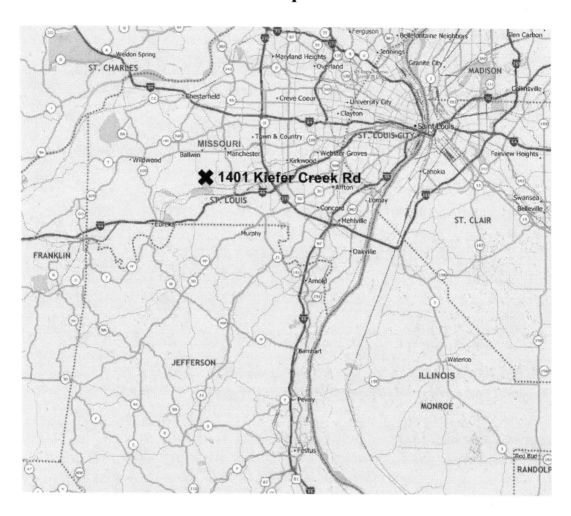

Creve Coeur Lake Memorial Park
Sailboat Cove - 13725 Marine 63146
Upper Park - 13236 Streetcar Drive 63043
(314) 615-4386

Park Hours
- 8 am to one half hour past official sunset.

Lengths
- Creve Coeur Connector: 2.5 miles
- Meadows Loop Trail: 2.5 miles
- Mallard Lake Loop Trail: 2.5 miles
- Lakeview Loop Trail: 3.5 miles

Amenities
- Playground
- Spray Fountain Play Area
- Trails
- Disc Golf
- Archery
- Tennis Courts
- Fishing
- Restrooms

Fun Fact
- Creve Coeur Park is the largest park consisting of 2,240 acres. The Park takes its name from the French words "broken heart."

Trails

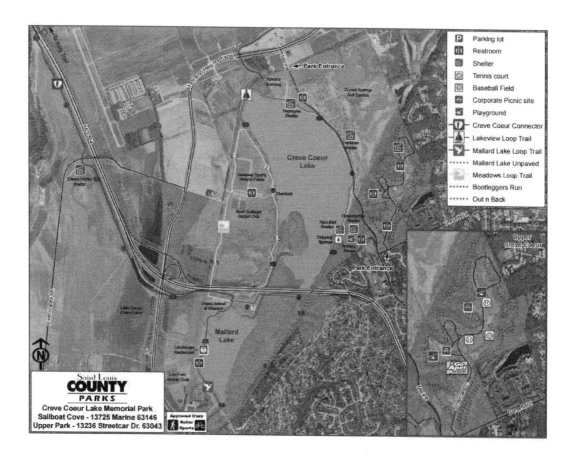

Creve Coeur Lake Memorial Park Pictures

A small fitness trail that loops around Creve Coeur Lake.

Creve Coeur Lake.

Map

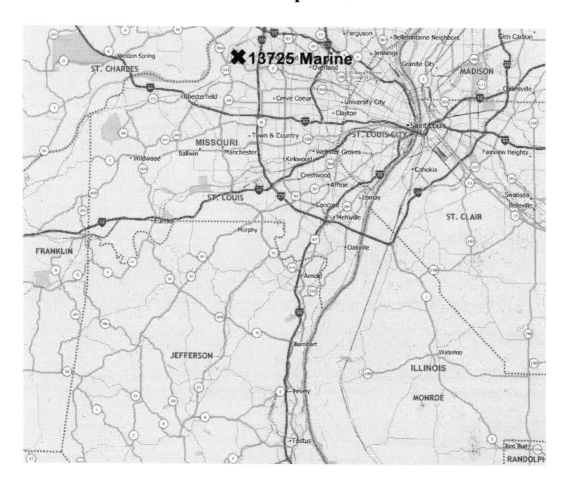

Dr. Edmund A. Babler Memorial State Park

800 Guy Park Drive
Wildwood MO 63005
636-458-3813

Park Hours
- Summer Hours (April through October) - 7 am to 9 pm, daily.
  Winter Hours (November through March) - 7 am to 6 pm, daily.

Lengths
- Dogwood Trail: 2 miles
- Equestrian Trail: 6 miles
- Hawthorn Trail: 1.25 miles
- Paved Bicycle Path: 1.75 miles
- Virginia Day Memorial Trail: 1.5 miles
- Woodbine Trail: 2 miles

Amenities
- Bathrooms

Fun Fact
- In 1934 Jacob and Henry Babler presented the state with 88 acres of land in loving memory of their brother Edmund, a prominent St. Louis surgeon, to make a park that would last for generations.

Trails

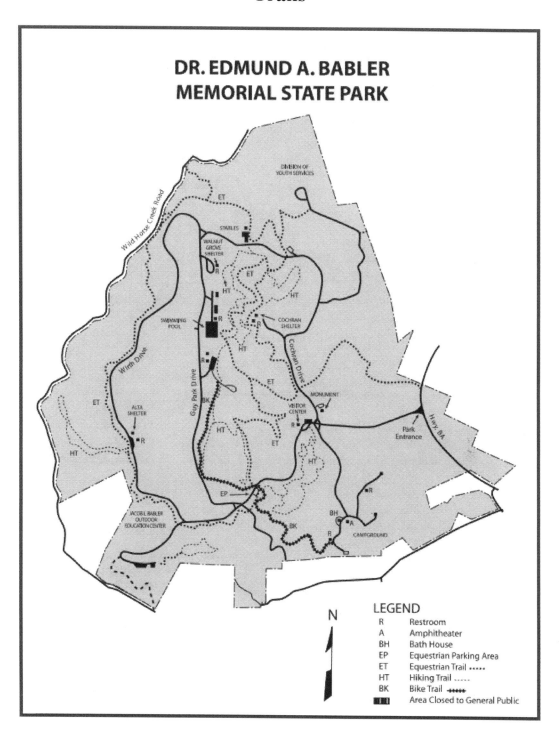

Dr. Edmund A. Babler Memorial State Park Pictures

When visitors enter the park they are greeted with an informational area which holds park maps and other information.

A lovely statue of Dr. Babler overlooks the park.

Map

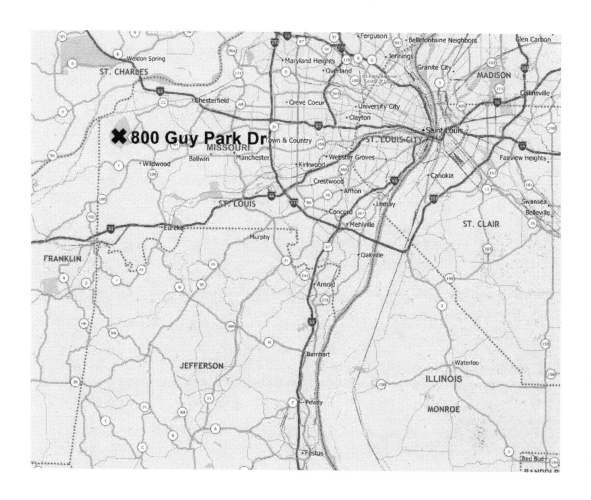

Emmenegger Nature Park
11991 Stoneywood Dr
St. Louis, MO 63122
(314) 822-5855

Park Hours
- 8 am-6 pm and 8 am-8 pm during daylight saving time.

Lengths
- Spur Trail: 0.0625 miles
- Bluff Creek Trail: 1 mile
- Main Lot Trail: 0.5 miles

Amenities
- Pavilions
- Bathroom

Fun Fact
- This land used to be privately owned by a real estate developer, who then donated part of his land to the city of Kirkwood.

Trails

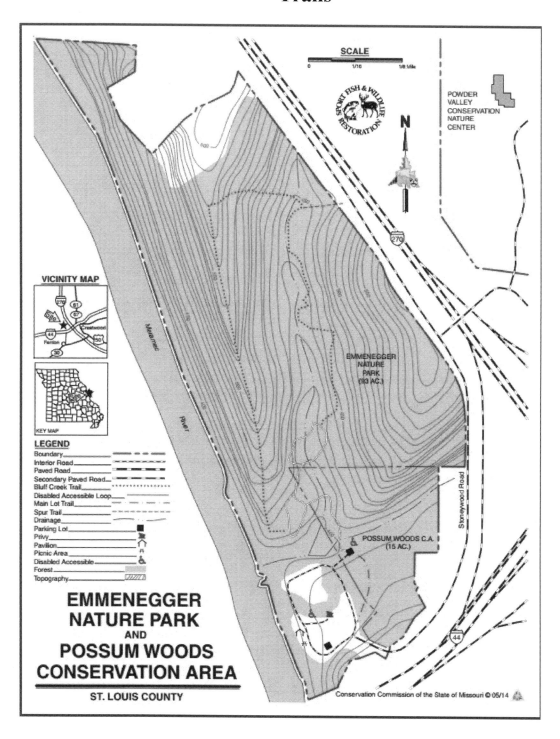

Emmenegger Nature Park Picture

The entrance to one of the several wonderful trails offered at Emmenegger Nature Park.

Map

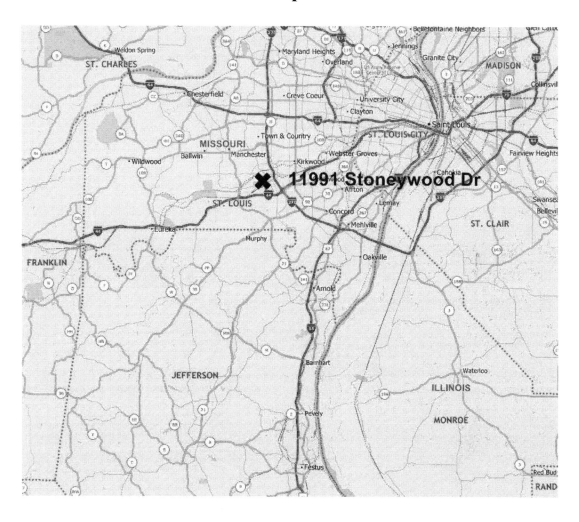

Faust Park
15185 Olive Boulevard
Chesterfield, MO 63017
(314) 615-8328

Park Hours
- 7 am to one half hour past official sunset.

Length
- Governor Bates Trail: 1 mile

Amenities
- Restrooms
- Historic Village
- St. Louis Carousal
- Butterfly House
- Pavilions

Fun Fact
- Faust County Park is located on a tract of land that once belonged to the second governor of Missouri, Frederick Bates.

Trail

Faust Park Pictures

One of the many butterflies featured in Faust Park's famous Butterfly House.

A beautiful day observing the scenery at Faust Park.

Map

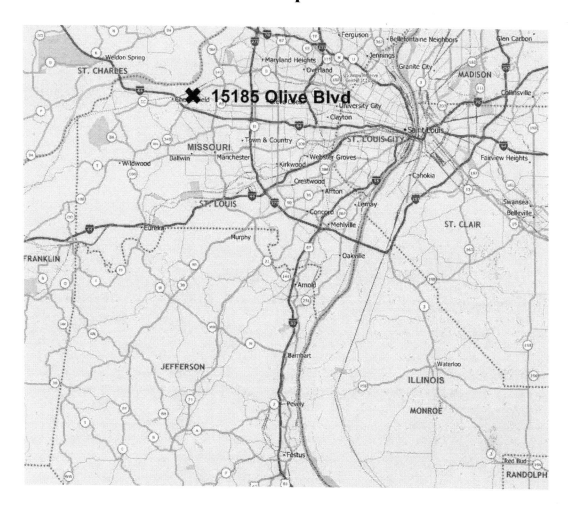

Fort Belle Fontaine Park

13002 Bellefontaine Road
Saint Louis, MO 63138
(314) 544-6224

Park Hours
- 8 am to one half hour past official sunset.

Length
- Fort Belle Fontaine Trail: 3 miles

Amenities
- Tour of the Fort
- Photo Gallery
- Historical Museum
- Bathroom

Fun Fact
- Lewis and Clark visited this area twice on their journey; once in 1804 and once in 1806.

Trail

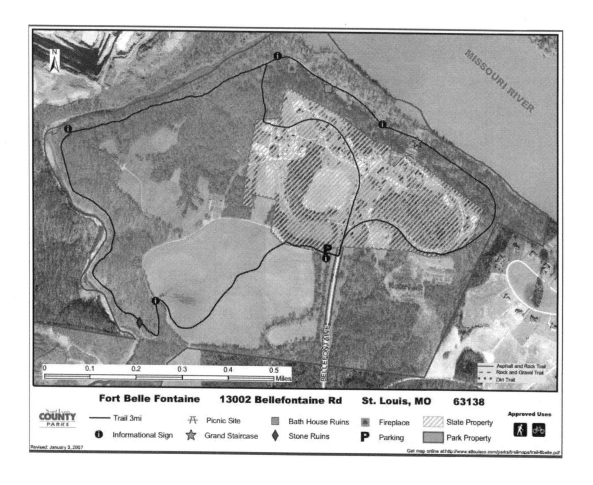

Fort Belle Fontaine Park Pictures

One of the many historical buildings the visitors can walk through.

Old remains overlook the stunning river.

Map

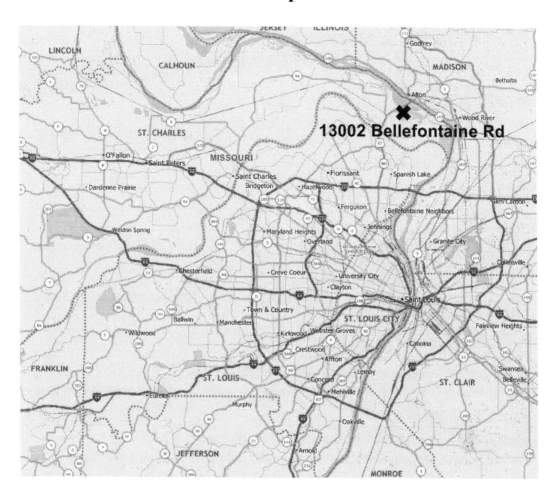

Greensfelder Park
4515 Hencken Road
Saint Louis, MO 63069
(314) 615-7275

Park Hours
- 8 am to one half hour past official sunset.

Lengths
- Green Rock Trail: 14.5 miles
- Beulah Trail: 2.1 miles
- DeClue Trail: 8.2 miles
- Deer Run Trail: 2.8 miles
- Dogwood Trail: 2.6 miles
- Eagle Valley Trail: 3.6 miles
- Mustang Trail: 1.7 miles
- Overlook Trail: 0.8 miles

Amenities
- Playground
- Nature Learning Center
- Restrooms

Fun Fact
- This park used to be a popular site for mining.

Trails

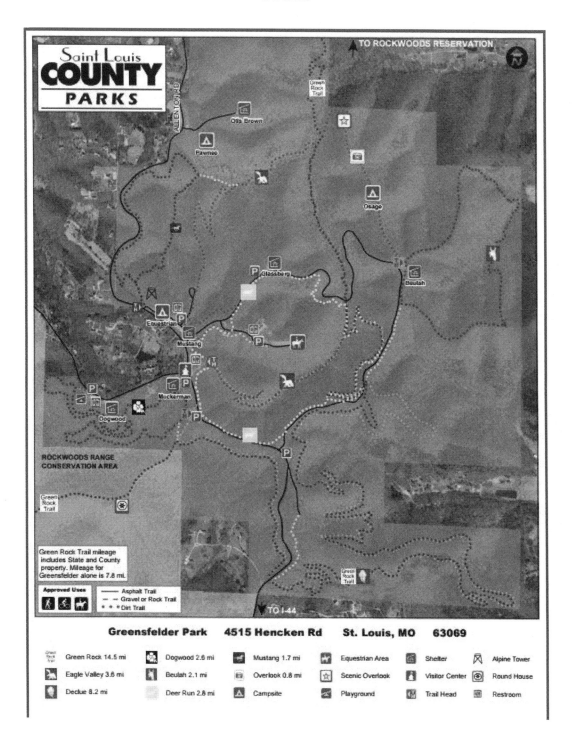

Greensfelder Park Pictures

The entrance to a couple of the trails featured at Greensfelder, which has 8 trails!

Trail markers are set throughout the trail to keep visitors safe and on the right path.

Map

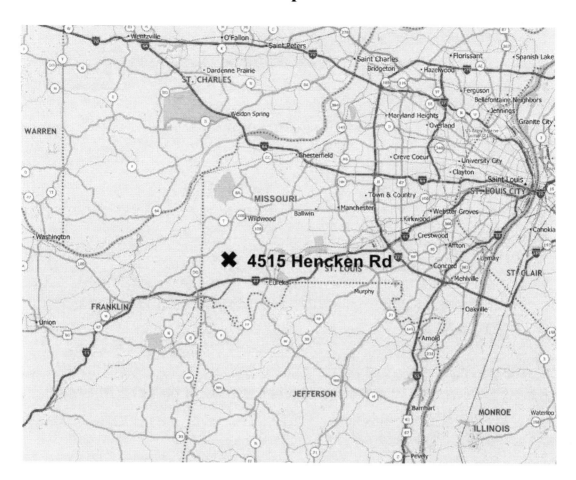

Laumeier Sculpture Park

12580 Rott Rd.
St Louis, Missouri 63127
(314) 615-5278

Park Hours
- 8 am to one half hour after official sunset.

Length
- Over 2 miles

Amenities
- Sculptures
- Bathrooms
- Education Center
- Stage

Fun Fact
- The concept of a sculpture park began with the offer of Ernest Trova to make a gift of large sculptures in 1975.

Trails

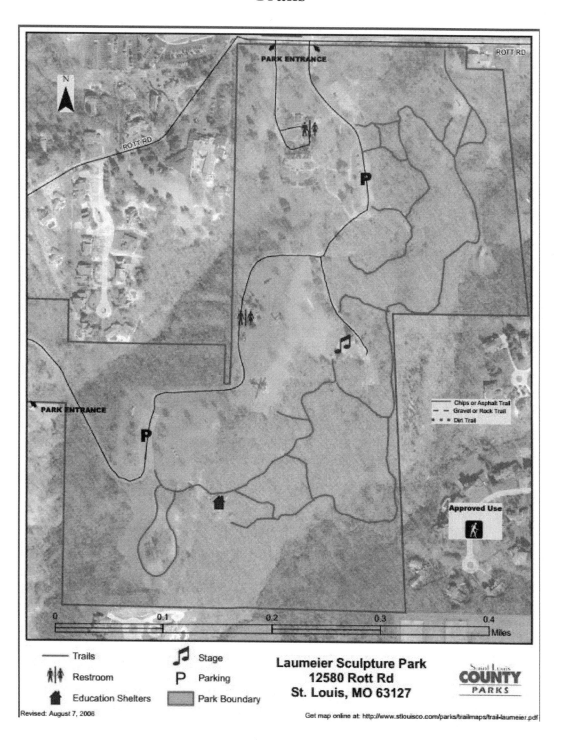

Laumeier Sculpture Park Pictures

The entrance to Whitaker Nature Trail, which is part of the Laumeier Sculpture Park.

One of the many unique sculptures featured at Laumeier.

Map

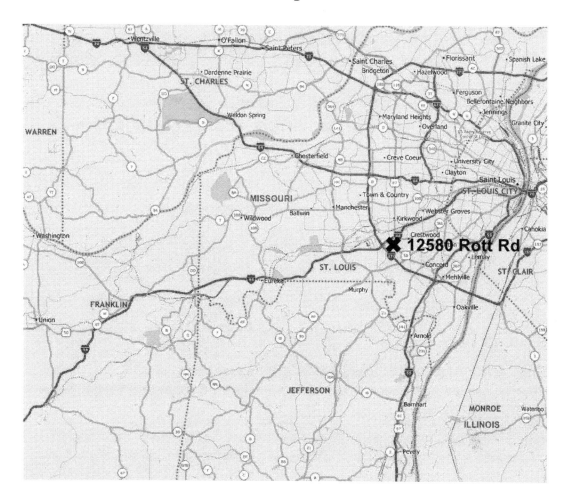

Lone Elk Park

1 Lone Elk Park Rd
Saint Louis, MO 63088
(314) 615-5000

Park Hours
- 8 am to one half hour past official sunset.

Length:
- White Bison Trail: 4 miles

Amenities
- Visitor Center
- Restroom
- Observation Tower

Fun Fact
- As you drive through the park you will notice the large observation tower, the 3 different bullet traps, and other left over structures of a by-gone era.

Trail

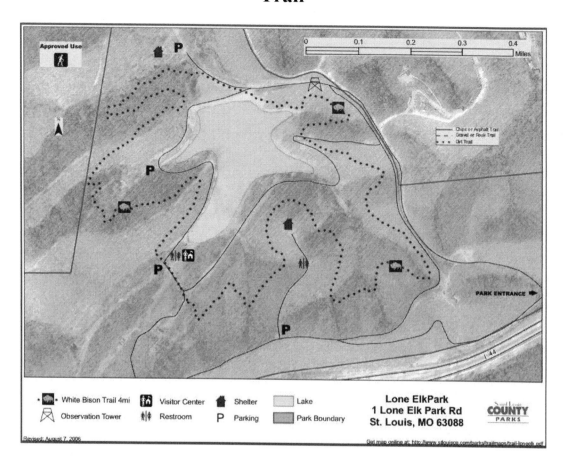

Lone Elk Park Pictures

A gorgeous look at the scenery of Lone Elk Park.

A trail marker on White Bison Trail.

Map

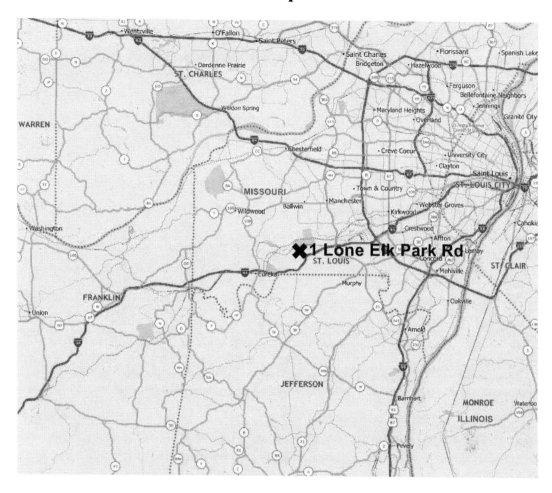

Love Park
2239 Mason Lane
Saint Louis, MO 63021
(314) 615-4386

Park Hours
- 8 am to one half hour past official sunset, except when reservations are issued.

Length
- Chipmunk Trail: 1.2 miles

Amenities
- Playground
- Restrooms

Fun Fact
- The two picnic shelters are named after the Love family children.

Trail

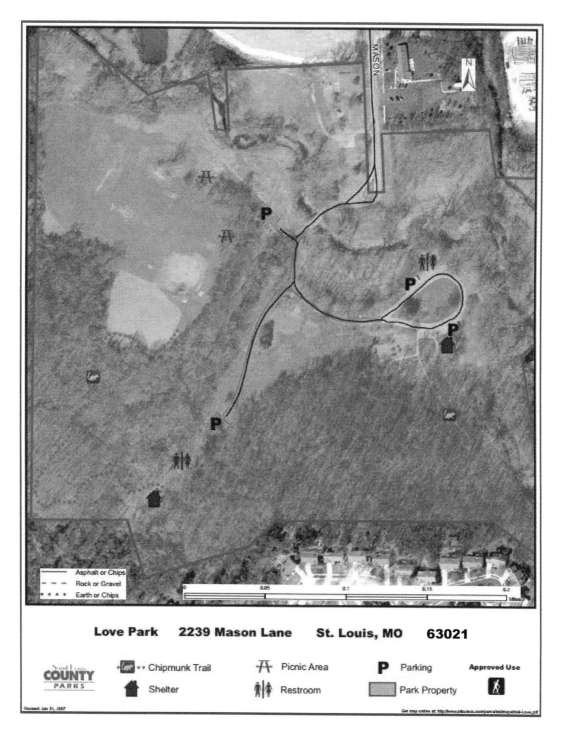

Love Park Pictures

A picture of the famous Chipmunk Trail, a landmark of Love.

The entrance to Chipmunk Trail as well as wonderful sitting area.

Map

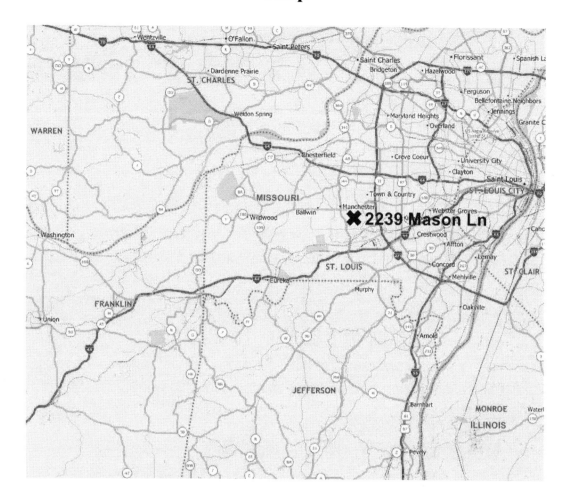

Mastodon State Park

1050 Charles J. Becker Drive
Imperial, MO 63052-3524
(636) 464-2976

Historic Site Grounds
- 8 am to one-half hour after sunset, daily, year-round.

Historic Site Office
- 9 am to 4:30 pm, Monday through Saturday; 12 pm to 4:30 pm, Sunday
- There will be times when the office is temporarily closed while staff members are working on the grounds. The office telephone is monitored for messages during office hours.

Museum Hours
- March 16 through Nov. 14; 9 am - 4:30 pm, Monday-Saturday; 12 pm - 4:30 pm, Sunday (closed Easter Day).
- Nov. 15 through March 15; 11 am - 4 pm, Monday; Closed Tuesday-Thursday; 11 am - 4 pm, Friday and Saturday; 12 pm - 4 pm Sunday
- Closed New Year's, Thanksgiving, and Christmas days

Length
- Limestone Hill Trail: 2 miles
- Spring Branch: 0.8 miles
- Wildflower Trail: 0.4 miles

Amenities
- Historic Site Museum
- Picnic Area

Fun Fact
- The park is home to many ice age deposits of fossils, including giant mastodons.

Trails

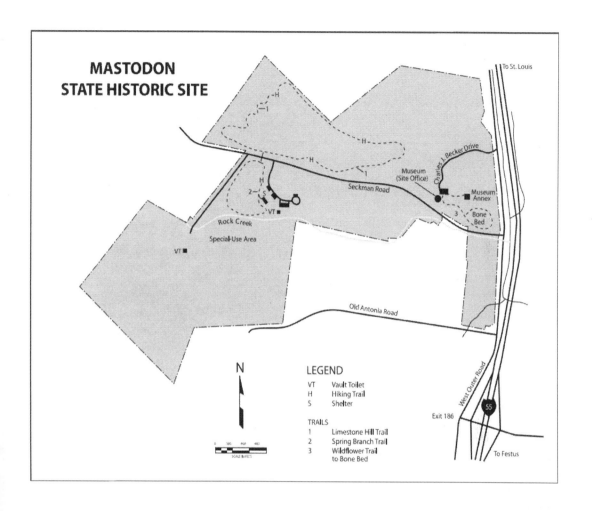

Mastodon State Park Pictures

The Historic museum where the Mastodon's bones are kept in preservation.

A trail mark of one of Mastodon's park trails.

Map

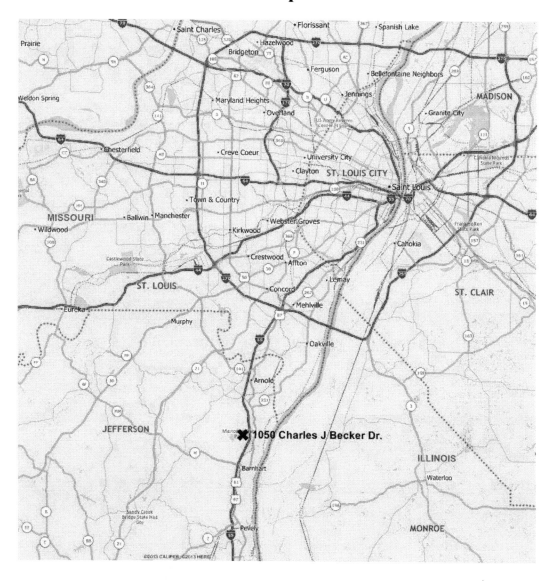

McDonnell Park
2961 Adie Road
Saint Louis, MO 63074

Park Hours
- 8 am to one half hour past official sunset.

Length
- McDonnell Trail: 1.6 miles

Amenities
- Playground
- Bathrooms
- Pavilions

Fun Fact
- The park was originally referred to as the Adie Road park site.

Trail

McDonnell Park Picture

McDonnell Park Trail encompasses the entire park. With a variety of fitness equipment dispersed throughout, you won't leave disappointed.

Map

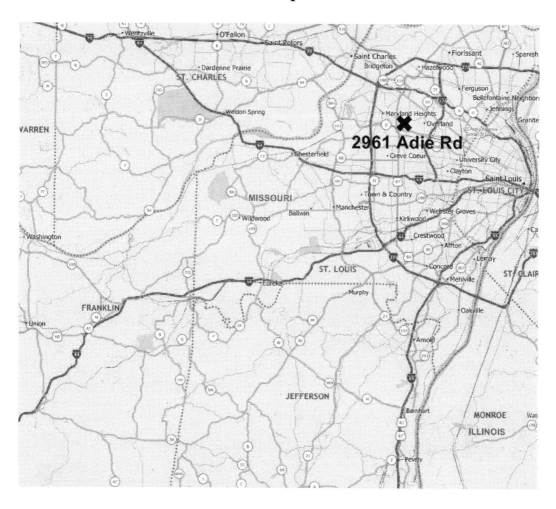

Montauk State Park

345 County Road 6670
Salem, MO 65560-9025
Park Office: (573) 548-2201
Lodging: (573) 548-2434
Store/Dining: (573) 548-2434
Nature Center: (573) 548-2225

Park Hours
- 24 hours a day
- Quiet Hours: 10 pm to 6 am

Park Office Hours
- Summer Hours (On-Season); March 1 through October 31 - 8 am to 4:30 pm, Monday through Sunday.
- Winter Hours (Off-Season); November 1 through February 28 - 8 am to 4:30 pm, Monday through Friday (with the exception of state holidays).

Lengths
- Montauk Lake Trail: 0.8 miles
- Pine Ridge Trail: 1.5 miles

Amenities
- Fishing
- Campsites
- Full Service Restaurant

Fun Fact
- Montauk State Park is one of the premier trout-fishing destinations.

Trails

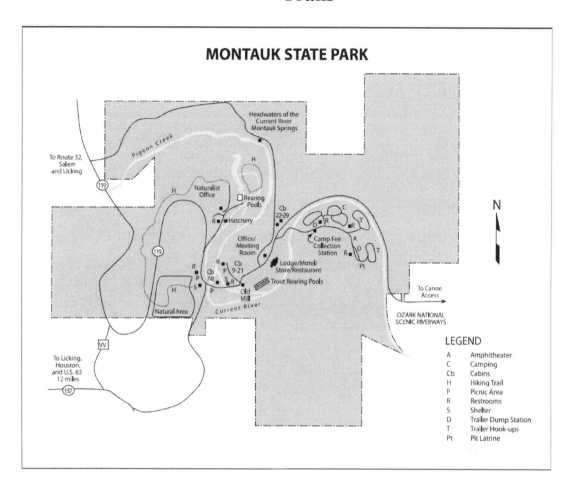

Montauk State Park Pictures

The river is a great place for fishing.

Map

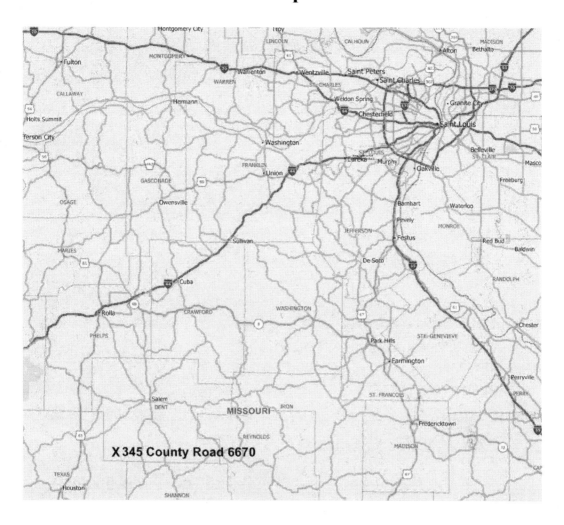

Powder Valley Conservation Nature Center
11715 Cragwold Rd.
Kirkwood, MO 63122
314-301-1500

Park Hours
- Open daily from 8 am to 8 pm during daylight saving time, and 8 am to 6 pm the rest of the year.

Lengths
- Broken Ridge Trail: 2/3 of a mile
- Hickory Ridge Loop: 1/2 of a mile
- Hickory Ridge Trail: 1 1/2 miles
- Tanglevine Trail: 1/3 of a mile

Amenities
- Conservation Center
- Gift Shop
- Pavilion
- Bathroom

Fun Fact
- During the Civil War, soldiers stored gun powder in the caves.

Trails

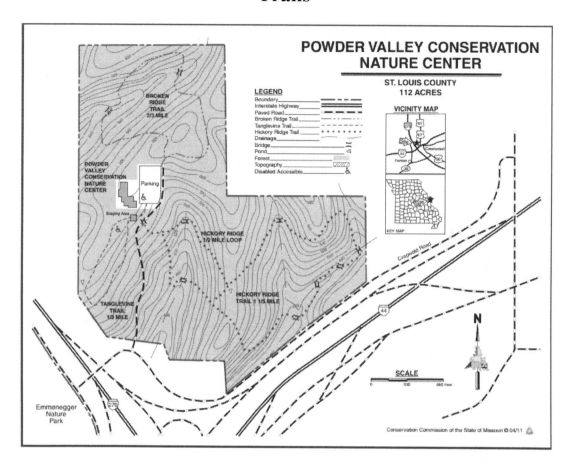

Powder Valley Conservation Nature Center Pictures

The Conservation Center, which has a small theater, is a great place for kids.

A bridge, which crosses over the entrance road, gives hikers a nice view.

Map

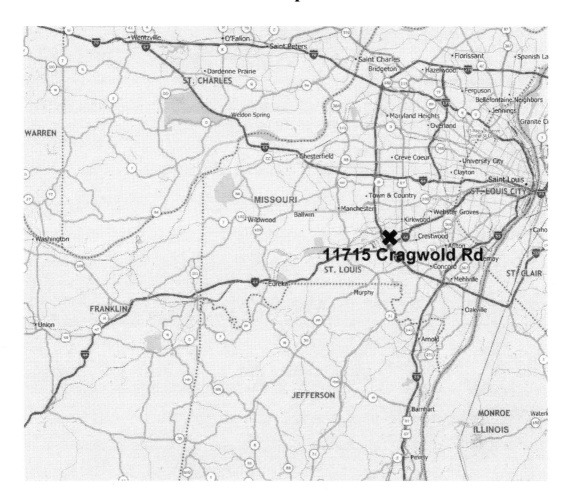

Queeny Park

550 Weidman Road & 1675 South Mason Road
Saint Louis, MO 63131
(314) 615-4386

Park Hours
- 8 am to one half hour past official sunset.

Lengths
- Hawk Ridge Trail: 4.4 miles
- Owl Creek Trail: 1 mile
- Fox Run Trail: 0.6 miles
- White Oak Trail: 0.6 miles
- Dogwood Trail: 0.4 miles
- Winding Hill Trail: 0.3 miles
- Pond Spur Trail: 0.2 miles
- Goose Trail: 0.2 miles

Amenities
- Restroom
- Dog Museum
- Fishing
- Recreation Complex

Fun Fact
- The Queenys sold their property to the American Investment Company Realty Corporation in 1964. St. Louis County purchased the property from the American Investment Company in March, 1970 for $3,310,000.

Trails

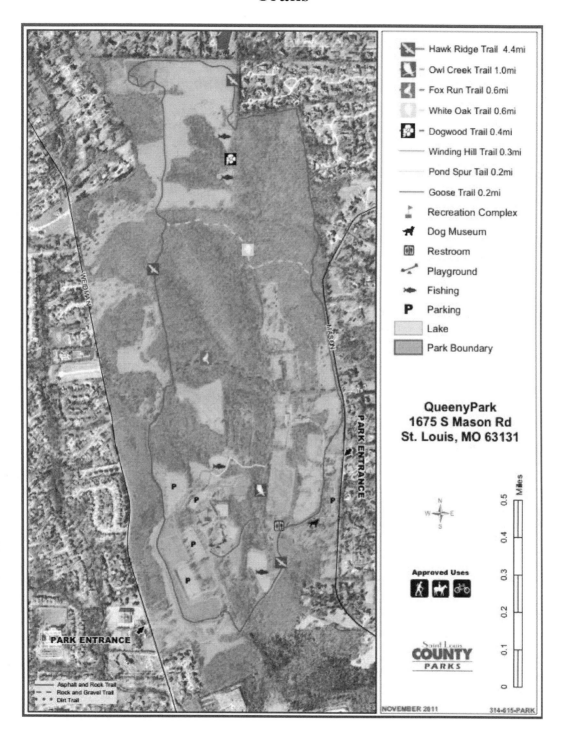

Queeny Park Pictures

A large playground for kids of all ages.

The entrance to one of Queeny Park's many trails.

Map

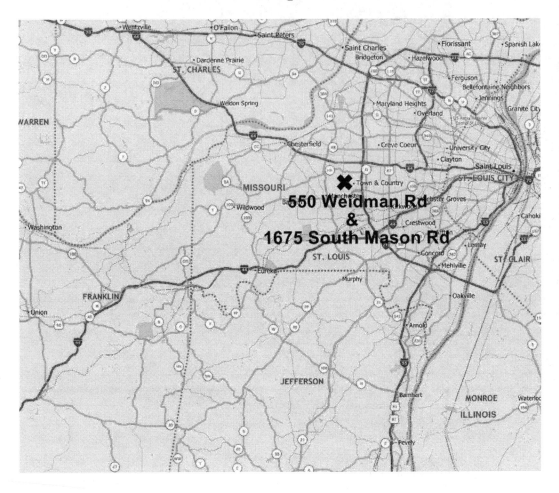

Robertsville State Park
900 State Park Drive
Robertsville, MO 63072
(636) 257-3788

Park Hours
- Summer Hours (On-Season); April through October; 7 am to 9 pm, daily.
- Winter Hours (Off-Season); November through March; 7 am to 6 pm, daily.

Boat Launch Hours
- On Season: 7 am - 9 pm
- Off Season: 7 am - 6 pm

Amenities
- Restrooms
- Camping
- Fishing
- Historic Site Tour

Fun Fact
- The park used to be a fully working farm in the early 1900s.

Amenities

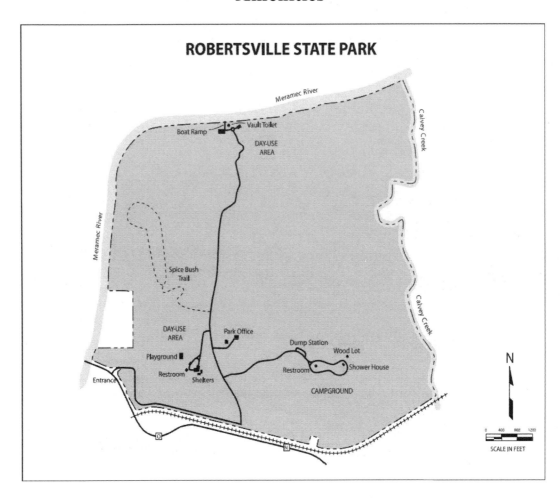

Robertsville State Park Pictures

The gorgeous pond featured at Robertsville State Park.

The entrance to the Roberts family cemetery.

Map

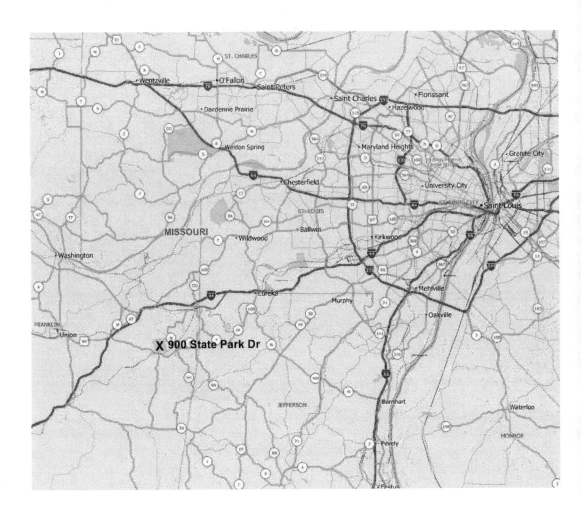

Route 66 State Park
97 North Outer Road
Eureka, MO 63025
(636) 938-7198

Park Hours
- 7 am to one-half hour after sunset, daily, year-round.

Boat Launch Hours
- 7 am to one-half hour after sunset, daily, year-round.

Visitor Center Hours
- March through November; 9 am - 4:30 pm daily
  - Closed Thanksgiving day
- December through February
  - Closed

Length
- Outer Loop Trail: 3.5 miles

Amenities
- Restrooms

Fun Fact
- The visitor center used to be a former hotel called the Bridgehead Inn.

Trail

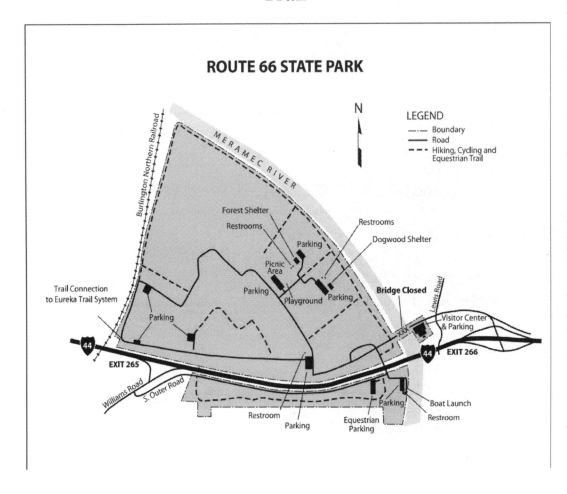

Route 66 State Park Pictures

A beautiful sitting area located in a meadow
with a wonderful view of the surrounding area.

A large trail that can be driven through, but is also used for hiking and general fitness.

Map

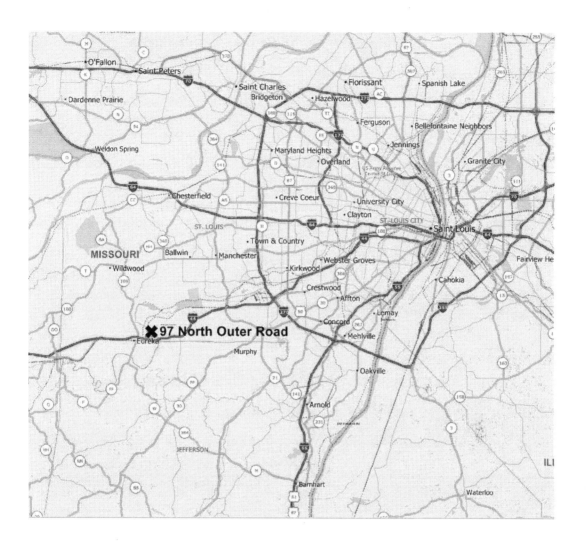

Simpson Park
1234 Marshall Road
Saint Louis, MO 63088

Park hours
- 8 am to one half hour past official sunset.

Lengths
- Blue Heron Trail: 0.8 miles
- River Walk Trail: 11.8 miles

Amenities
- Playground
- Fishing Dock
- Shelter
- Restrooms

Fun Fact
- The main attraction to the park is a 72 acre lake. The lake was created by the dredging of sand and gravel prior to park ownership.

Trails

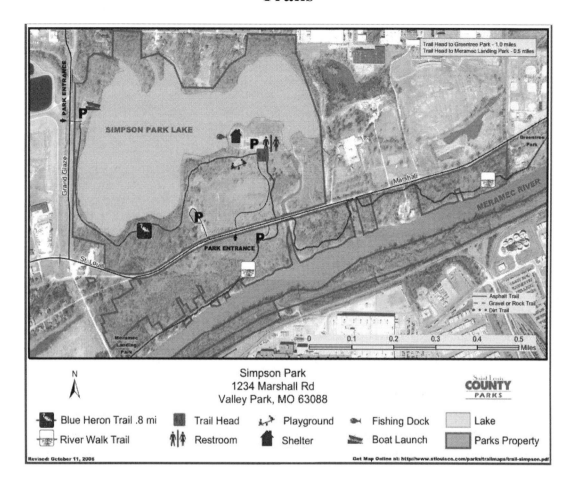

Simpson Park Pictures

The playground is a pleasant place for families to gather.

The trails at Simpson Park are not only beautiful but are great for biking too.

Map

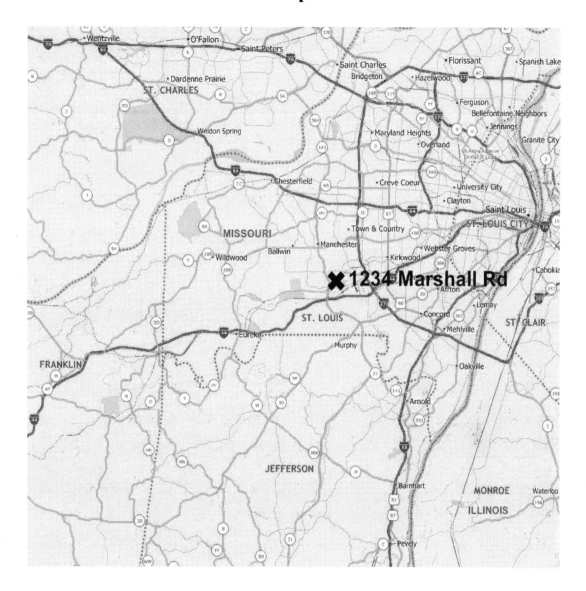

Spanish Lake Park
12636 Spanish Pond Rd
St Louis, MO 63138

Park Hours
- 8 am to one half hour past official sunset.

Lengths
Lakeside Trail: 1.6 miles
Spanish Trace: 1.9 miles

Amenities
- Restrooms
- Pavilions
- Playground
- Tennis Courts
- Fishing

Fun Fact
- During the early 1900's, the lake was a popular fishing destination.

Trails

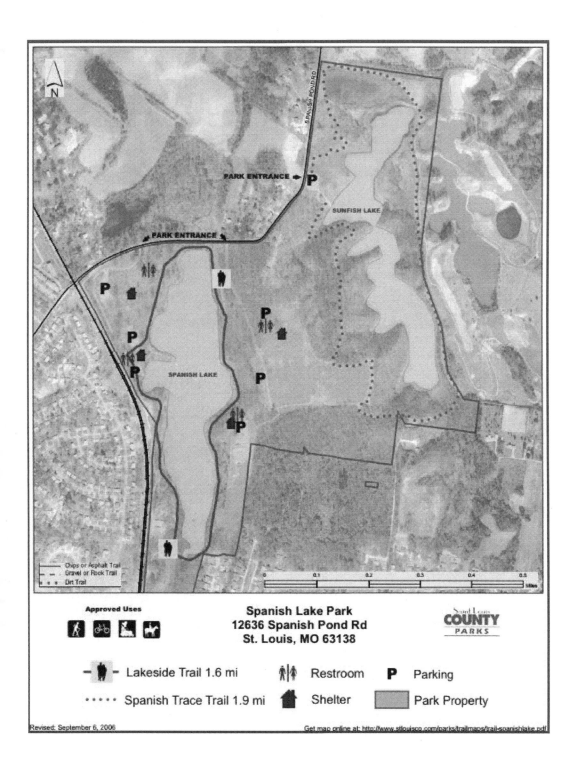

Spanish Lake Park Pictures

The lake is a great place to fish, and attracts visitors everyday.

The trails, while long, have delightful views such as the lake and trees.

Map

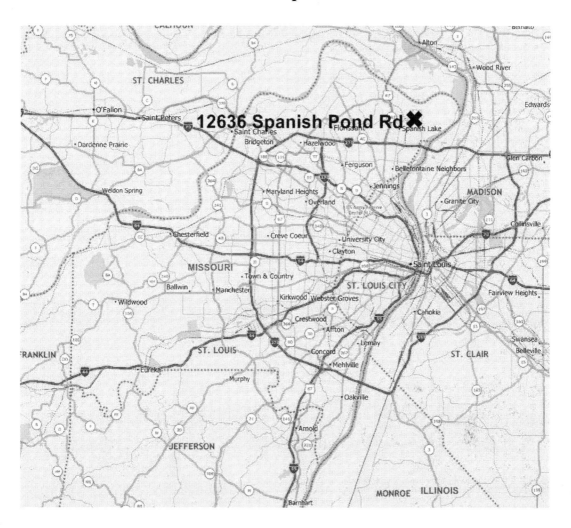

Stacy Park
9750 Old Bonhomme Road
Olivette, MO 63132
(314) 993-0444

Park Hours
- 8 am to 5 pm

Length
- Walking Path: 0.6 Miles

Amenities
- Restrooms
- Fitness Path
- Playgrounds
- Pavilions
- Barbecue Pits

Fun Fact
- The park is home to Olivette's Fall Celebration.

Trail

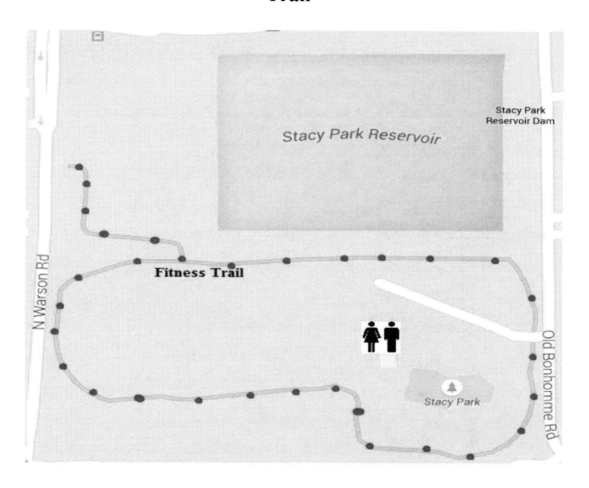

Stacy Park Pictures

The swing is a great place to rest and enjoy the scenery.

Map

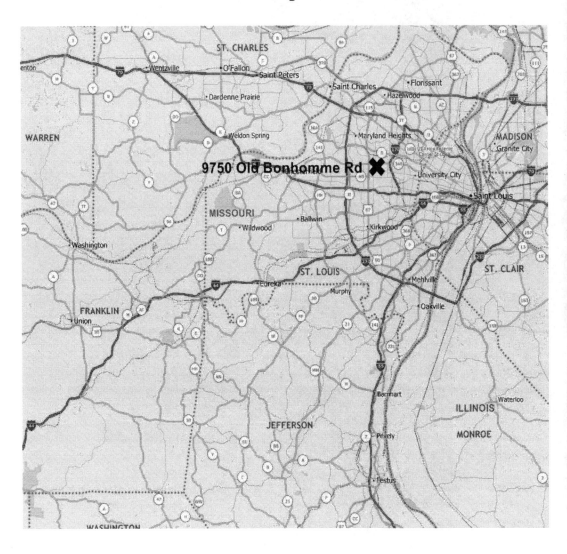

Unger Park
500 Yarnell Road
Saint Louis, MO 63026
(314) 615-8484

Park Hours
- 8 am to one half hour past official sunset.

Length
- Meramec Greenway: 1 mile

Amenities
- Fishing
- Shelter

Fun Fact
- The land for the park was donated by the Alberici Company in 1974 in conjunction with the Land and Water Conservation Fund Grant.

Trail

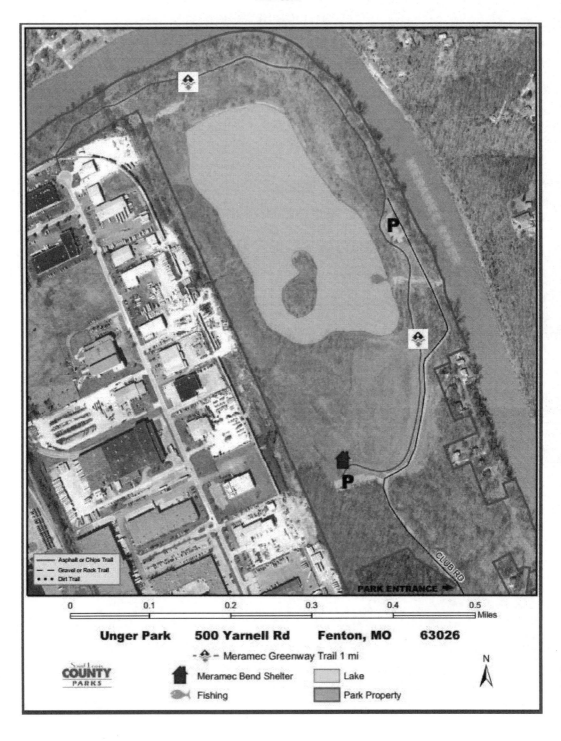

Unger Park Pictures

The bike trail runs around the lake at Unger Park.

The pavilion at Unger Park overlooks the lovely lake, giving visitors a perfect place to hold activities.

Map

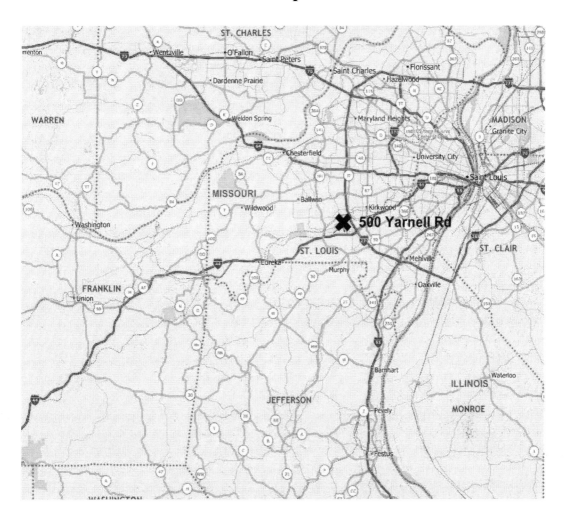

West Tyson Park
131 North Outer Road East
Saint Louis, MO 63025
(636) 938-5144

Park hours
- 8 am to one half hour past official sunset.

Lengths
- Chubb Trail: 7 miles
- Flint Quarry Trail: 3 miles
- Chinkapin Trail: 0.5 miles
- Prairie Loops: 1.5 miles
- Low Water Route: 0.9 miles
- Connector Trail: 0.5 miles
- Castlewood Loop: 2.8 miles

Amenities
- Bathroom
- Pavilions
- Picnic Area

Fun Fact
- Famous among prehistoric Americans as a place where the highest quality flint for arrowheads could be obtained. These flint quarries still exist today.

Trails

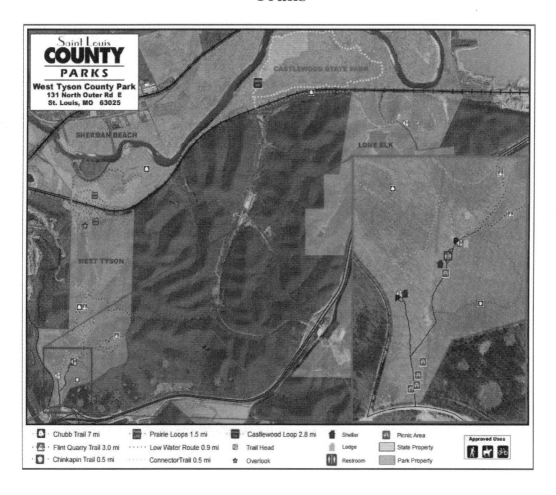

West Tyson Park Pictures

A trail along West Tyson gives walkers a wonderful view of nature.

A trail marker guides hikers along the trails.

Map

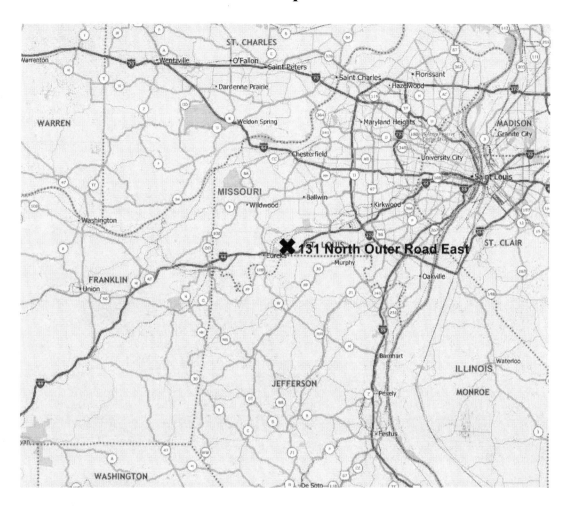

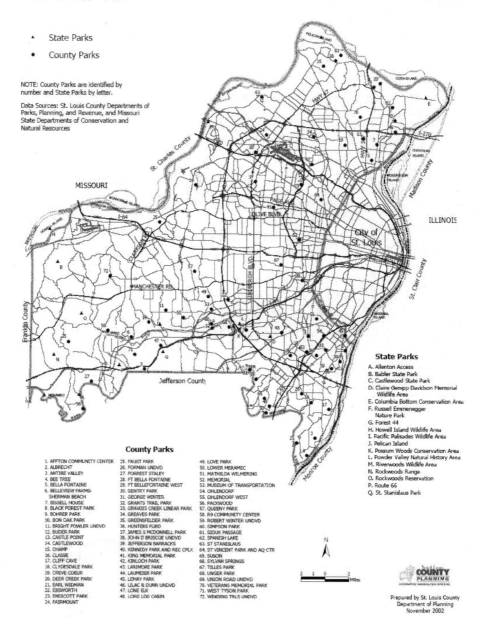

Hiking Equipment Checklist

- ✓ Appropriate clothing
- ✓ Canteen or water bottle
- ✓ Cell phone
- ✓ Day pack
- ✓ Emergency shelter such as an ultra-light tarp, emergency space blanket, or plastic trash bag
- ✓ Extra clothing according to the season
- ✓ First aid kit
- ✓ Flashlight or headlamp and extra batteries
- ✓ Good hiking shoes
- ✓ Hat or bandana
- ✓ Insect repellent
- ✓ Map and compass
- ✓ Matches and fire starters
- ✓ Pocketknife
- ✓ Quality socks and spare pairs
- ✓ Rain gear
- ✓ Sun protection
- ✓ Toilet paper and hand sanitizer for longer hikes.
- ✓ Trail food
- ✓ Whistle and/or signaling mirror

Made in the USA
Lexington, KY
08 June 2018